CRAFTY CATS

CRAFTY CATS

Jan Eaton · Caroline Green · Sue Quinn

HPBooks
a division of
PRICE STERN SLOAN
Los Angeles

The copyright on craft designs featured in this
book belongs to the authors: Jan Eaton, Caroline
Green and Sue Quinn.

Published by HP Books, a division of Price Stern Sloan, Inc.,
360 North La Cienega Boulevard, Los Angeles, California 90048.
Printed in Belgium.

9 8 7 6 5 4 3 2 1

Library of Congress Cataloging-in-Publication Data

Eaton, Jan.
    Crafty cats / by Jan Eaton, Caroline Green, and Sue Quinn.
        p.   cm.
    Includes index.
    ISBN 0-89586-825-3: $12.95 ($14.95 Can.)
    1. Handicraft.   2. Cats in art.   I. Green, Caroline (Caroline M.)
II. Quinn, Sue.   III. Title.
TT157.E27   1989
745.5—dc19   88-37112
                                                              CIP

Editor: Jilly Glassborow
Designer: Glynis Edwards
Photographer: Steve Tanner
Color artwork: Malcolm Porter
Typeset by: SX Composing Ltd., England
Color separation by: Fotographics Ltd., London – Hong Kong
Printed by: Proost International Book Production,
Turnhout, Belgium

CONTENTS

INTRODUCTION

Designed to appeal to lovers of cats and crafts alike, this delightful book will show you how to make over fifteen original cat designs, from appliquéd cushions and embroidered samplers to quilted velvet rugs and hand-knitted sweaters. And you don't even have to be experienced at needlecraft to make some of the projects – if your talents lie more towards painting and modelling, why not stencil a pretty cat border around your walls, make a novel mobile from modelling clay or delight your friends with your own handmade greeting cards and gift wrapping paper?

The picture below shows some of the many different materials used to make the designs in this book. The paints, brushes, sponges, masking tape, scissors, craft knives, wools, threads, needles, embroidery hoops, canvas, velvets and fur fabrics are all used in a wide range of crafts from painting and modelling to knitting, embroidery and soft toymaking.

Each project is illustrated with a sumptuous colour photograph and accompanied by detailed instructions showing you how to make it. And, though it would be impossible within the scope of this book to explain all the various techniques involved, there are plenty of hints and tips that will guide you towards achieving perfect results.

The embroidery designs, such as the delightful Literary Cats and jazzy Ginger Geometrics, are also accompanied by a stitch chart which you can follow square by square. Bear in mind that each square on the chart represents one stitch.

Many of the other projects feature a scaled down pattern of the design, drawn on a grid. The grid is there to help you reproduce the pattern full size using a method known as 'squaring up'.

Squaring Up the Design

On each pattern grid you will find the scale marked, for example one square represents 2.5cm (1in). Taking a sheet of paper, a felt-tip pen and a long ruler, draw your own grid to the dimensions indicated. Then choose a point on the pattern from which to start. Note which square it occupies and find the corresponding square on your own grid. See where the pattern outline enters and leaves the square and mark these points on your grid. Now join the two points, carefully following the shape of the outline within the square.

Continue to copy the pattern on to your grid, square by square. When you have finished the general outline, fill in the details such as eyes, mouth and other markings, paying particular attention to their positioning. Be sure, also, to mark the direction of pile arrows on each of the toy pattern pieces. This is very important as, if you eventually cut out the fur fabric with the pile running in the wrong direction, you will ruin the finished look of your toy.

If you wish to make your design larger than the suggested size, simply draw your squares bigger; if you double the size of square you will double the size of pattern. Similarly, you can also reduce the final pattern size by drawing your grid smaller than suggested.

Using Your Pattern

For some projects we suggest you use this squared up paper pattern for creating the design; you can either cut it into individual pattern pieces, as for the appliqué work, or trace off it – see the roller blind on page 17. For other projects, such as the three soft toy designs, we suggest you make cardboard templates of the pattern. These will last longer if you need to use them several times and you will find them easier to trace round than the paper patterns. (The fur fabrics used in toymaking are too thick to pin paper pattern pieces on to, so you have to use a felt-tip pen to trace the shapes directly on to the reverse of the fabric.)

Materials and Equipment

To help you prepare for making the various projects, we have, in each case, provided a list of the materials and equipment you will need. Always try to buy good quality materials, particularly fabric and wools, because, though they may be more expensive than inferior products, the end results will be so much better. Similarly, always buy good quality paint brushes; if you care for them properly they should outlive any cheaper varieties. Wash them immediately after use in the appropriate solvent and allow them to dry in shape.

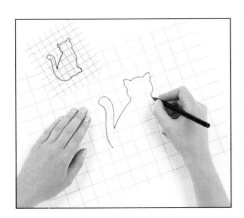

To reproduce a pattern to the correct size, first draw up a grid on a piece of paper to the size indicated. Then copy the outline very carefully, one square at a time, on to your grid.

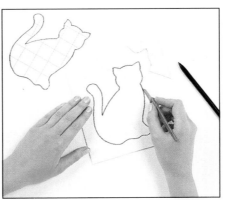

If you need to make your pattern more hardwearing, make a template of the design. Cut out the paper pattern and trace round the outline on to a piece of cardboard. Now cut the template out.

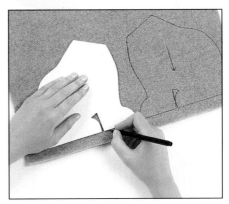

When making soft toys, use your cardboard template to trace the pattern pieces on to fur fabrics. If two asymmetrical pieces are required, turn the template over before tracing the second piece.

CRAFTY CARDS AND GIFT WRAPS

Here are some delightful ideas for making your own personalized greeting cards. You can even make colourful gift tags and wrapping paper to coordinate with one of the designs.

Embroidered Good Luck Card

Send 'Good Luck' wishes to a special friend with this prettily embroidered card. It is worked on even-weave fabric in cross stitch (see page 39) and is the ideal way to use up any oddments of stranded cotton thread you may have.

The embroidery has been made to fit a card blank with a circular aperture measuring 8cm (3in) across. (Card blanks are readily available from good craft suppliers.) It was stitched on a 12cm (5in) square of cream 14-gauge 'Aida' fabric using a range of attractive colours.

First, stretch the fabric in a hoop to help keep the stitching neat and even. Then find the centre block on the fabric and mark it with a pin. Find the corresponding square on the chart (right) and begin to stitch the design square by square, working outwards from the centre. Use three strands of thread, and remember that each square on the chart represents one cross stitch worked over one block of fabric.

When the design is complete, remove the hoop and press the embroidery on the wrong side, taking care not to flatten the stitching. To finish the card, cut away the surplus fabric from round the edge of the embroidery, allowing a margin of 2cm (¾in) all around. Position the embroidery in the window, turn the card face down and secure on the wrong side with masking tape. Finally, glue the flap down over the back of the embroidery.

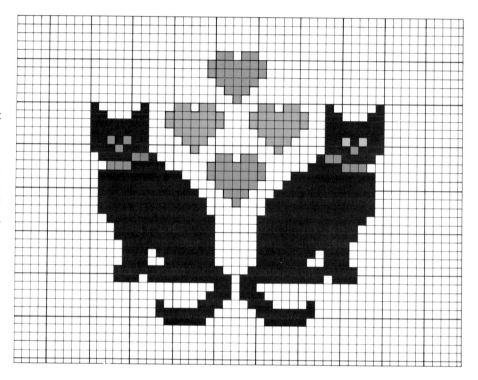

1 *Draw the cat outline on to the cut potato with a felt-tip pen. Cut along this line, holding the knife vertically. Now trim off the excess potato from around the outline to leave the cat shape as a flat raised area.*

2 *Mix up the required colour and paint it generously on to the cat shape only. Turn the potato over and print on to clean paper. If you press fairly hard you should get three progressively paler images from each coating of paint.*

Cat-Through-the-Window Card

To make this charming card, you will need a photograph of a cat, either taken from your own photo album or cut from a magazine or calendar. In the latter case, choose a picture on good quality paper so that any print on the reverse side will not show through. The size of your cat picture will determine the size of the piece of cardboard and shape of window that you will need.

Place a piece of tracing paper over the cat picture and draw a window slightly smaller than the size of the picture. Trace the window on to a large piece of white or coloured cardboard and cut out the window panes with a craft knife. Cut along the inner edge of the window frame and score the card at the sides, using the back of a craft knife, to make hinges so that the windows will open and close. Draw the outline of the outer frame and sill in black.

Fold the cardboard in half to form the card, with the window on the front and the fold on the left. Carefully glue the cat picture behind the window, on the inside flap of the card, then trim off any excess cardboard so that the window is in the centre.

This is your full size cat outline. Use it to make a potato cut for printing the cards, tags and wrapping paper.

Rainbow-Cat Paper and Tags

This jolly wrapping paper is quick and easy to make and works out much cheaper than buying paper and tags from a stationer's. First make a tracing of the cat shape on the left. Transfer this on to thin cardboard and cut it out with a craft knife to make a template for drawing around. Take a medium-sized potato and cut it in half; then, following steps one and two on the opposite page, use your template to make a potato cut.

We used all the colours of the rainbow and printed rows of cats diagonally across a large sheet of thin white paper to make the wrapping paper. Use artists' acrylic paints or poster paints and a small brush. Print a few cats singly on to another sheet of paper for cards and tags. Experiment with paint colours, sometimes mingling two shades on one print for variety.

When the paints are dry, use the all-over printed paper to wrap your presents and then complete the picture with a toning satin bow. To make the tags, cut out one cat shape and glue it on to a rectangle of white cardboard. Fold the card in half and make a small hole in one corner for a length of narrow ribbon or cord.

To make the greeting card, cut out a single cat shape, glue it on to a square of coloured cardboard and then mount it on to a piece of white folded cardboard to complete. Alternatively, you can buy a card blank from a craft shop and glue your cat print inside the aperture.

PAPA MÂCHÉ AND FAMILY

*T*his fun family of cats is made of papier mâché moulded around party balloons. You can display the cats as ornaments, or, using a little ingenuity, fill them with sand and transform them into paperweights. Alternatively, before painting them, you can cut a slit in the top and turn them into novelty money boxes – an ideal gift for a child.

out any joints showing. Hang the balloon up with a clothes peg to prevent the papier mâché from sticking to the work surface while it is drying.

Next follow step four to prepare the cat for painting. When the coats of gesso are complete, burst the balloon with a pin and pull the pieces out through the hole in the bottom. You will be left with a slightly ragged edge to the papier mâché here, so trim this level using scissors or a craft knife so that the finished cat will stand upright. You can leave the base open or cover the hole with strips of glued paper and a coat of gesso. This latter step will be necessary if you want to make your cats into paperweights or money boxes.

Painting Your Design

After you have completed step four you will need to work out the surface design. You can either use our cats as reference, or, if you prefer, search for design inspiration in gift shops and magazines, or on birthday cards. Draw your design on to the papier mâché model in pencil.

There are several methods of making papier mâché, but the version we describe here is probably the least messy and gives a good smooth result, although it does take quite a while to build up the various layers.

Follow steps one and two as described on the opposite page and continue building up to about four layers of paper. Now make the ears as shown in step three and position them on the head. Leave the model to dry after this until it sounds hard when you tap it. Then build up about four more layers so that the model feels quite firm and the ears blend into the general shape with-

1 *Blow up a balloon and knot it about 6cm (2½in) from the open end, so that only the top part of the balloon is inflated. Smear the whole surface with petroleum jelly to prevent the paper adhering permanently.*

2 *Tear a large piece of lining paper into small scraps. Dilute the glue with a little water in a saucer. Using a brush dipped in glue, pick up the scraps of paper and paste them on to the balloon, covering the surface completely.*

3 *For the ears, cut out two 6cm (2½in) diameter paper circles. Snip each circle to the centre and fold it into a cone shape, gluing to secure. Snip around the base of each cone, stuff with tissue paper and glue in position.*

When you have finished, mix your paint colours carefully with a little water and paint in the large areas first. Leave details such as facial features, handkerchiefs, jewellery and buttons unpainted at this stage.

When the paint is dry, use a smaller brush and fill in the detail on the face and clothing. Use a fine black felt-tip pen for delicate lines such as the whiskers and the type on the newspaper. To get the fur texture use a little thick paint applied sparingly with a dry brush or dab the paint on with a small moist sponge. Now paint stripes in various shades over the base colour.

Leave the paint to dry and then apply a protective sheen with one or two coats of varnish, using either gloss or semi-matt as you wish.

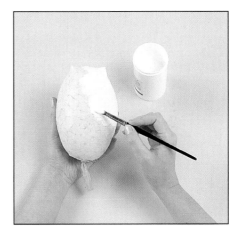

4 *When the papier mâché is quite hard, paint all over with gesso. Leave to dry, then sand lightly to smooth out any bumps. Repeat this process with more coats of gesso and a final sanding to prepare the surface for painting.*

Left: Don't forget to paint the back of your cats, allowing their tails to peep through the clothing as we have here.

Fat Cat Border

This delightful border of fat felines will brighten up any child's room. Stencil it at picture rail or dado height, and repeat the design on a piece of furniture for perfect coordination.

Stencilling is a simple and quick way to reproduce a motif an indefinite number of times without variation. The colour is applied through cut-out shapes in a cardboard or acetate stencil which is taped in position on the wall or furniture.

Before you begin stencilling your walls make sure the surface is clean, free of grease and smooth. A plain matt finish

This is your full size stencil pattern. Trace the dotted guidelines as well as the solid cutting lines as these will help you position the stencil correctly each time.

As an alternative to soft pinks and greys, try colouring the cats in bolder shades to create a more striking effect, ideal for a kitchen or breakfast room.

on walls provides a good background for a stencil border. Alternatively, a slightly broken colour such as a subtly dragged or ragged paint finish can look particularly effective.

Fast drying stencil paints, readily available from craft shops, make stencilling quick, clean and easy but there are other materials such as stencil

You will need:
Fast drying stencil paints
Stencil brushes
Acetate stencil sheet
Masking tape
Fine black waterproof felt-tip pen
Craft knife
Cutting board or thick cardboard
Scrap paper
White mounting cardboard
Pencil and rubber
Long ruler
Kitchen paper

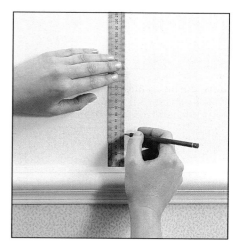

1 *Referring to the design provided on page 12, cut out an acetate stencil sheet, making it about 10cm (4in) larger all round than the motif. Use masking tape to hold the sheet in place centrally over the design and then carefully trace off the solid outlines and all the dotted guidelines using a waterproof felt-tip pen.*

2 *Place the acetate stencil sheet on a flat surface or cutting board and, using a craft knife, carefully cut out the design, following the solid outline. If you intend to use two or more colours in your border, as we have, you can make a separate stencil for each colour, cutting out only the relevant areas on each one.*

3 *Using a soft leaded pencil, lightly mark a base line or top line around your wall, measuring carefully to ensure that it runs parallel to your dado rail, picture rail, door frame or whatever. Attach the stencil in position with masking tape, lining up the dotted line with the pencil line on the wall.*

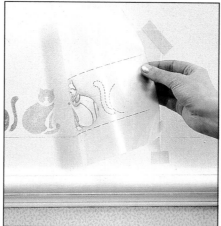

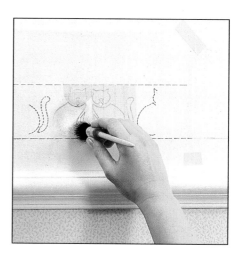

4 *Pour a little stencil paint into a saucer. Dip the brush into the paint and dab it on to some dry kitchen paper. Test the brush on a scrap of paper and, when the paint stops looking blotchy, begin to work on the stencil using a light circular movement, going first in a clockwise and then in an anti-clockwise direction.*

5 *Lift the stencil away from the wall occasionally to check your progress. When all the shapes have been filled in to your satisfaction, carefully lift off the stencil and reposition it over the next area to be painted. Match the dotted lines over the previous stencil motif in order to keep the designs evenly spaced.*

6 *For a multi-coloured design, as an alternative to making several stencils you can use a single one and mask off unwanted areas with tape. Always finish one colour before you reposition the mask and begin to stencil the next colour, and remember to allow the paint to dry between coats to avoid smudging.*

crayons, aerosol spray paints and emulsion paints that work well when applied with a small natural sponge. There are also special fabric paints now on the market which allow you to stencil curtains, cushions and clothes too.

Practise First

When you have cut your stencil according to steps one and two opposite, take some time to practise the technique before tackling a real wall. Also try experimenting with various combinations of colour and arrangements of the motifs. Use white mounting cardboard for your experiments and write a little note near each piece of stencilling to remind you of the colour and methods used, for future reference. Try shading your design with more colour at the base and down one side to give the image a three-dimensional look. A little lighter colour can also be used for highlighting. Try blending a second colour over the first as well, allowing time between applications for the paint to dry.

Planning the position of your design on the wall is very important. Measure up and mark the walls lightly in pencil before you begin, spacing out the design and fitting it around windows or up a stair rail. You can always rub the pencil marks out afterwards. When you come to painting the border, try to arrange the motifs so that they fit neatly around corners without breaking the design.

For a more sophisticated effect, use this full size pattern to create an Egyptian-style cat border, suitable for a dining room, hall or sitting room.

The 'Egyptian' motif works well with the cats stencilled in alternate colours; or why not try using it in an undulating pyramid pattern for a wide border at picture rail height? You will need to make a different stencil for the latter design, positioning the cats as shown below and adding dotted guidelines above and below.

A ROOM WITH A VIEW

*T*ry your hand at painting this original trompe l'oeil roller blind, complete with a cat sitting on the window sill. It's a great deal easier than you'd think using a ready-made roller blind and some ingenious painting techniques such as sponging and potato printing, so that even a novice can achieve wonderful results.

You will need:

A plain white or cream roller blind to fit your window
Artists' acrylic paints in various colours
Acrylic medium for thinning paint
Brushes (oil painting and water-colour)
Small real sponges
Masking tape
Large sheet of paper for pattern
Potatoes
Pencil
Small kitchen knife
Black waterproof felt-tip pen
Long ruler

Choose a roller blind, preferably spongeable, with a smooth or slightly linen texture, which is ideal for painting on. Draw out the design to fit your blind on to a large piece of paper (such as wall lining paper) referring to the pattern on page 19. Note that each square represents 10cm (4in). Use a black waterproof felt-tip pen to draw the pattern so that it will show up through the blind fabric.

Now follow step one on page 18, tracing the main parts of your design on to the blind. Don't draw round all the leaves as you may want to vary these shapes as you print the foliage. Leave the paper pattern underneath the blind afterwards to guide you as you paint.

Follow steps two and three, then mask around and paint the large areas of sky and garden in the background, carefully easing the masking tape around any curved areas. To thin the paints, mix them with acrylic medium rather than water, as very watery paint may make the blind fabric stretch slightly and then go bumpy as it dries. Use a sponge or large oil painting brush to paint large areas and use the paint sparingly. Change to a small moistened sponge to dab darker green paint on to the blind to make the hedges and bushes.

Now follow steps four, five and six to make the potato cuts and print the leaves and flowers. Lastly, mask around the cat and paint it a light gingery brown all over. Very lightly outline the main stripes and use chestnut brown paint on a moistened sponge to fill them in. Add more, darker stripes over the top. To complete the cat, remove the masking tape and draw in a set of fine whiskers with a sharp pencil.

The various paint techniques used provide an interesting range of textures and effects. A set of delightful whiskers, drawn in pencil, add the final touch.

1 *Lay the roller blind over your pattern and hold it in place with masking tape. Lightly pencil in the main features such as the window frame, garden and cat.*

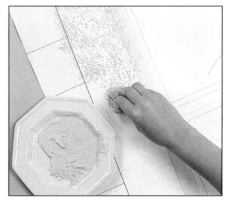

2 *Remove the tape holding the pattern, then mask off the outer edge of the window frame. Dab the surrounding area with a moist sponge dipped in paint.*

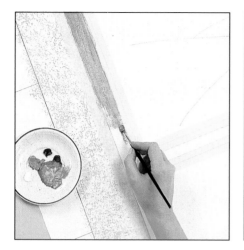

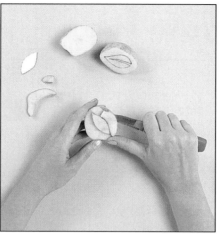

3 *When the paint is dry, mask around the window frame. Mix some paints with acrylic medium to make the colour of stripped pine. Using a dry oil painting brush, paint the window frame, dragging the paint in lines to resemble wood grain. Next, mask around and paint other areas – such as the sky, hills and lake.*

4 *To print the foliage, first cut a potato in half and dry the surface. Using a cardboard template made from one of the leaf shapes below, trace a leaf on to the cut surface of the potato. Cut vertically into the potato, following this outline, then cut away the excess potato from the edges to leave a flat raised leaf shape.*

5 *Mask off the painted window frame with several widths of tape. Mix up a soft green colour and paint some on to the leaf shape, then press the potato cut on to the blind. Continue to print leaves, using a range of greens and overlapping the shapes to give a natural effect. Then use a fine brush to paint the leaf stems.*

6 *Make some geranium flower and leaf potato cuts in the same way and use them to print the geranium plant. Also paint a few buds and stems using a brush. When this is dry, mask and paint the pot in shades of terracotta using a larger brush. Finally, mask and paint the cat, finishing off with a fine set of whiskers.*

Use these full size shapes to make potato cuts for printing the leaves and flowers on to your roller blind. Trace them directly from here and then turn the shapes into cardboard templates.

One square represents 10cm (4in)

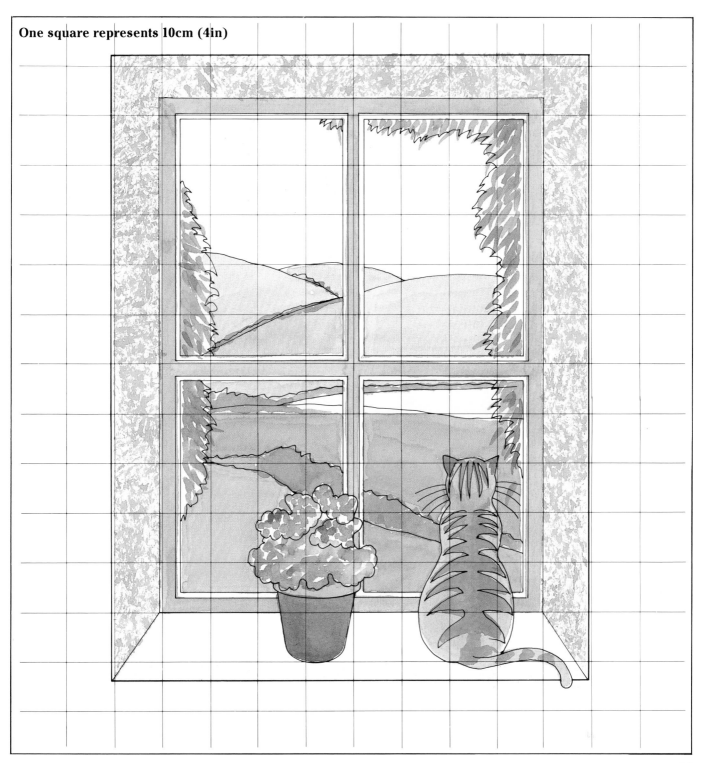

CRAZY CAT MOBILE

*T*his enchanting mobile will delight cat lovers of all ages – and even kittens! It's easy enough for the children to make, though they may need a little help with the cutting out and baking.

We've used a self-coloured modelling material called Fimo to make this unusual mobile. It's readily available from most art and craft shops and is both clean and easy to mould. And to harden it you simply bake it in the oven. It comes in a wide range of colours, so you can choose whether to make your mobile in natural cat shades, as we have here, or in vibrant reds, blues and yellows. Alternatively, you could use the same cat shapes to make badges; just glue a brooch fastening on to the back after the cats have been varnished.

Select your colours and follow steps one, two and three to make up to 12 cats. Using the template as a guide, make a small hole in the top of each one so that you can thread cord through later. The hole is slightly off-centre so that the cat will hang straight.

Lay the cat shapes on to a clean baking sheet and cook for about twenty minutes in a pre-heated oven at 130°C/250°F/Gas Mk ½. Then remove the cats from the oven and leave them to cool on a flat surface.

You will need:

Fimo modelling material in a selection of colours
Fimo varnish
Fine cord
Lampshade ring, 20cm (8in) in diameter
Craft knife
Rolling pin
Greaseproof paper
Modelling tool
Narrow ribbon
Baking tray
Scissors
PVA glue
Water-colour brush
Thin cardboard

1 *To make the multicoloured cats, you will need to mix several colours of Fimo together. Break off a small piece of each colour and roll it into a long sausage shape. Twist these pieces together and gradually roll them into a ball. Continue to roll, stretch and fold the piece of Fimo until the colours mingle sufficiently to make a pleasant marbled pattern.*

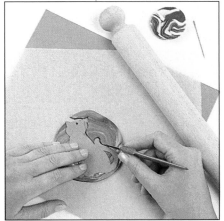

2 *Knead the Fimo until it is soft and smooth, and then roll it out to about 3mm (1in) thickness. Use greaseproof paper when rolling out to prevent the Fimo sticking to the rolling pin or work surface. Lay the cat template on top of the Fimo and cut round it carefully with a craft knife. Remove the surplus material and carefully peel off the template.*

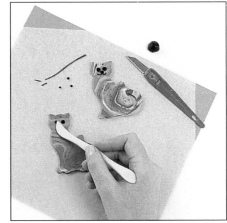

3 *Roll three tiny balls of black Fimo for the eyes and nose. Roll another piece into a long thin sausage shape and cut off two pieces about 1.5cm (⅝in) long. Place the eyes in position on the cat and press flat with a Fimo modelling tool. Curve the two long pieces into a mouth shape and add the nose. Flatten as before and repeat on the reverse side.*

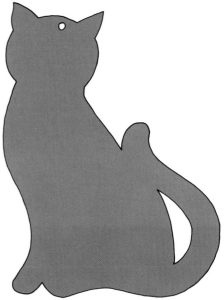

This is your full size pattern for the mobile. Trace it from here and transfer the shape on to a piece of thin cardboard. Then cut it out to use as a template.

Once cool, varnish the hardened cat shapes on both sides and leave them to dry. The varnish will help to bring out the colours and provides a strong protective coating. You can use either gloss or matt varnish, as you prefer.

Constructing the Mobile

Thread lengths of cord through the holes in the top of each cat. Make a knot at the end and dab on a little glue to anchor the knot just inside the hole. Tie the cats at various heights on to a lampshade ring, forming a pleasing arrangement. Be sure to space the cats out evenly so that the ring hangs level.

To hide the cord knotted around the ring, bind the ring with narrow ribbon. Wind the ribbon round and round, over-lapping the layers slightly, and glue the end to finish. Tie a piece of cord on to the ring for hanging the mobile and adjust the position of the knots so that the mobile hangs level.

COSY QUILTED RUG

Made out of luxurious cotton velvet and quilted for comfort, this cosy cat rug will encourage everyone to sit around the fire on a winter's evening. Use rich autumnal shades for added warmth or, if you prefer, choose softer pastel colours to match the decor of your room.

This delightful project combines the popular crafts of quilting and appliqué to give a beautifully soft rug. We've chosen a mixture of russet browns, chestnut and camel to resemble the patterned fur of a ginger cat. To make it perfectly practical, it's all made in cotton furnishing velvet which is both hard-wearing and dry cleanable.

Velvet needs careful handling when making up. Remember that it frays easily once cut, so handle it as little as possible. The layers also tend to slip somewhat, so tack (baste) the pieces together carefully before machining, rather than relying on pins alone. Also, you shouldn't iron velvet in the normal way as the pile marks very easily. You can buy a special velvet board for pressing, though we found ironing was not necessary for this project.

Creating the Design

First draw up your full size pattern, copying the design on page 25. Then trace out the individual pattern pieces on to thin pattern paper. Follow step one on page 24 for cutting out the shapes in fabric. You may find it advisable to number each pattern piece to help you place them correctly later on. If so, leave the pattern paper pinned in place on the fabric until you come to step two.

Follow steps two and three, then try out your machine satin stitch on some spare scraps of velvet and wadding.

To make the satin stitch, set the machine to a very close, medium-width zig-zag stitch. You will need to make the stitches as close together as possible so that the raw edges of fabric are well covered to prevent fraying and give a neat finish to your work. As you sew, ensure the fabric is feeding through the machine correctly by adjusting the pressure on the presser foot. This will vary according to the thickness of fabric and the number of layers of fabric and wadding you are using.

Follow step four to sew the appliqué pieces in place and add the wadding. When you have completed the satin stitching you should pull all the end threads through to the back of the fabric. Knot them in pairs securely and trim off any excess thread. This neatens the back of your work and prevents the satin stitching coming undone.

The wadding will enhance the quilted effect. Lay the appliquéd cat shape on to a piece of wadding with the right side uppermost. Pin and tack (baste) the layers together to hold the wadding securely in place. Then zig-zag stitch all round the raw edge of the velvet to neaten and hold the wadding. Carefully cut away any excess wadding from around the edge, being careful not to cut the zig-zag stitching as you go.

Follow step five to make the quilting lines along the paws, whiskers, tail and features. Work from the centre of the rug, stitching out towards the edge, to avoid puckering the fabric. Finish off the lines of stitching, as before, by tying the threads securely together at the back.

You will need:

70cm (¾yd) of 122cm- (48in-) wide cotton furnishing velvet in russet brown for the main colour

30cm (⅜yd) of 122cm- (48in-) wide cotton furnishing velvet in camel colour

30cm (⅜yd) of 122cm- (48in-) wide cotton furnishing velvet in light brown

Scraps of velvet in dark brown for the eyes and nose

Scraps of orange chintz for eyes

70cm (¾yd) of medium weight terylene wadding

70cm (¾yd) of 122cm- (48in-) wide cotton drill backing fabric

Cotton sewing threads in dark brown, light brown, orange and russet brown

Scissors

Pins

Thin pattern paper

Black felt-tip pen

Making Up the Rug

Cut out a cat shape in cotton drill fabric and stitch this backing on to the appliquéd rug as described in step six. Then carefully trim away some of the fabric and wadding from the seam allowance, about 1cm (⅜in) away from the stitching, all around except for the opening. Snip a series of small V shapes into the remaining seam allowance so that the seam will lie flat when you turn the rug the right way out. Be very careful not to snip through the stitching as you do this.

Turn the rug through to the right side and flatten it out. Fold in the seam allowance along the opening and pin it in place. Finally, hand stitch the opening to complete the rug.

1 Pin the individual pattern pieces on to the appropriate coloured fabrics, ready for cutting out. For the main cat shape, cut the pattern piece 2cm (¾in) outside the outline to give a seam allowance when making up the rug. Cut out all the other pieces accurately along the outlines as these will be used for the appliqué.

2 Unpin the paper patterns and place each piece of fabric right side up on to the main cat shape. Refer to your pattern to check the exact positioning of each piece. (Don't pin the two pupils or the nose in position yet.) Tack (baste) around each piece, close to the raw edge, so that the layers will not slip when stitching.

3 Pin the nose and the two pupil pieces on to wadding to pad them slightly. Tack, then zig-zag stitch, all around the edge of each piece to hold the layers together. Carefully cut away the excess wadding around each piece, making sure you don't cut the stitching. Tack these pieces in position on to the cat.

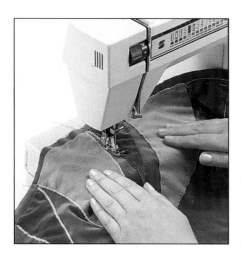

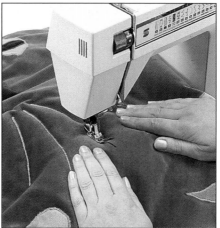

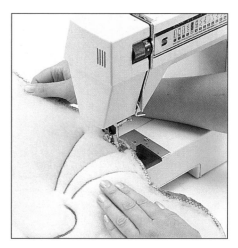

4 Set your sewing machine to a very close zig-zag stitch and carefully sew around the edge of each appliqué piece, making sure the stitches cover the raw edges. Change the colour of thread to blend with the eyes, nose and paws. Now cut out the cat shape in wadding and sew it on to the back of the velvet cat.

5 Using the pattern as a guide, carefully draw in the lines for the face, paws, and tail. If you like you can tack through the paper pattern as a guide. Use a felt-tip pen to mark the lines on to the velvet, then stitch along these lines with satin stitch, tapering the ends of the whiskers to make them pointed.

6 Using the main cat pattern piece, cut out a piece of backing fabric 2cm (¾in) outside the outline. Lay this piece on top of the appliquéd velvet, with right sides together. Tack in place all around the edge. Machine stitch 2cm (¾in) away from the raw edge and leave a gap about 30cm (12in) long for turning.

Left: If autumnal shades don't go with the colour scheme of your room, why not try this alternative and make a grey tabby instead of a ginger Tom. The design follows the same pattern as the original but uses different colours, so it's just as easy to make.

Below: Here is a scaled down pattern for the cat rug. Copy it square by square on to a full size grid as described in the introduction on page 7. To make the rug the correct size, each square on your grid should be 10cm×10cm (4in×4in).

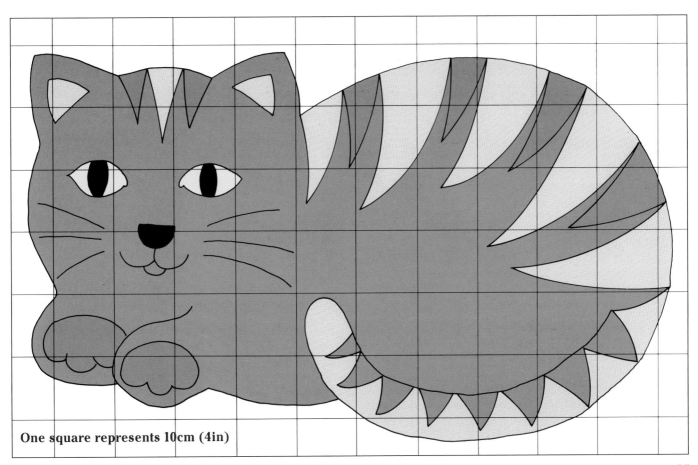

One square represents 10cm (4in)

SOPHISTICAT CUSHION

Go for the modern approach with this black and white cat cushion made in shiny chintz. It will blend with the most up-to-date furnishings and the simple appliqué technique can be worked on the sewing machine or by hand as you wish.

First, draw up the pattern from page 29, enlarging it as instructed in the introduction on page 7. Make each square of your grid 5cm×5cm (2in×2in).

Using some lightweight paper and your chintz fabric, follow steps one and two to make the cat's head and body as separate pieces. Then follow step three, adding wadding to the main shapes. This will give an attractive padded look to your cushion cover.

Sewing the Design
At this point you should decide whether to work your appliqué stitches by hand or on the sewing machine. The machine method is quicker but your sewing machine will need to have zig-zag stitch to do it. If it has, set the machine to a very close, medium-width zig-zag stitch. Try the stitch out first on some scrap material until you achieve just the right effect. You can adjust the stitch so that it looks almost like a smooth line of piping, or open it out a little so that you can just see the separate stitches.

For really good results it is best to use the same coloured thread on the top reel and on the bobbin, so always change both threads when you change colour.

Following step four, work all the inside lines of stitching and then sew around the outer edges to cover the ends of the previous rows of satin stitch. This

gives a very neat finish. To prevent any rows of stitching from coming undone, pull the threads through to the back of the work and knot them securely, then cut off any loose ends.

Working by Hand
If you prefer to work by hand you should use stranded cotton embroidery threads in the appropriate colours instead of ordinary cotton sewing threads. Use a buttonhole stitch to work around the edge of each shape, completely covering the raw edges and stopping the fabric from fraying. For details such as the eyes and whiskers use satin stitch, gradually tapering it to a point where necessary. Both these stitches are described fully on page 43.

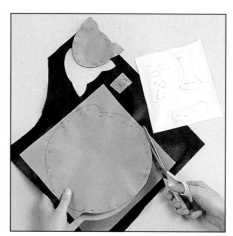

1 *Trace off each pattern shape separately on to some lightweight paper. Then pin the head, body and nose on to the black chintz and the eyes, tail, face panel and ears on to the white chintz. Cut out the pieces carefully. Also cut out two circles of white chintz 36cm (14in) in diameter for the cushion back and front.*

2 *Iron the bonding web on to the reverse side of the eyes, ears, face panel, nose and tail pieces. Trim away the excess webbing, following the outline of the fabric. Peel off the backing paper and, referring to the pattern, position the shapes on to the head and body. Iron in place to bond the fabrics together.*

Making Up the Cushion Cover

When you have finished the appliqué stitching you will need to make your cat up into the cushion cover. Follow steps five and six to make a length of decorative striped piping and stitch it on to the edge of the cushion cover front.

Now place the cushion back over the front piece, with right sides together and raw edges matching all round. Pin and then tack (baste) in position round the edge. Still using the zipper foot, machine stitch the pieces in place, close to the piping cord leaving a gap of about 25cm (10in) through which you can insert the cushion pad.

Trim away the raw edges of the seam allowance, close to the stitching, and turn the cover the right way out. Press the cover if necessary, then insert the cushion pad and hand stitch the opening to neaten. Instead of sewing the gap closed you could insert a zip in the opening so that the cover can be removed more easily for laundering.

If you prefer, you can make the cushion in a softer colour scheme, such as the one shown below. Here, we suggest using beige and brown chintz to make a Siamese cat. The cover can be made using pale blue to match the colour of the cat's eyes.

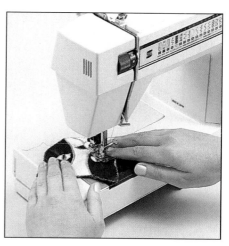

3 *Pin the head and body shapes on to pieces of lightweight wadding to pad them. Zig-zag stitch all round the edges of both pieces to keep the layers in place and to neaten the raw edges. Very carefully trim away the excess wadding all round each piece, being very careful not to cut the stitching as you go.*

4 *Using a machine satin stitch, first sew the eye centres in black and green. Then change to a pale grey thread and stitch round all the features. Tack (baste) the body to the cushion front and satin stitch all round, following the tail and leg shape. Finally, satin stitch the head in position and sew the whiskers.*

5 *Iron the striped fabric and fold it diagonally to find the bias. Cut along the fold to make 6cm- (2½in-) wide strips. Join the pieces, right sides together, to make a piece about 120cm (47in) long. Fold round the piping cord, with right side outside, and pin. Stitch close to the cord using a zipper foot on the machine.*

6 *Tack the covered piping cord, as shown, round the edge of the cushion front, matching up the raw edges. Where the ends meet, cut away the piping cord from inside the fabric covering. Flatten the striped fabric and overlap the raw ends. Finish tacking and then machine stitch all round, close to the piping cord.*

One square represents 5cm (2in)

GINGER GEOMETRICS

*S*titch a cheerful ginger cat in brightly coloured wools on canvas to make a stylish but hardwearing cover for a drop-in chair. To ensure the cover will be a perfect fit on your own chair, measure the seat carefully, allowing an extra 1cm (½in) of embroidery where the seat fits into the chair to avoid any unworked canvas showing.

EMBROIDERY STITCHES

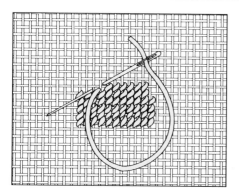

Tent Stitch
Work tent stitch in horizontal rows, starting at the right of the shape and working the rows in an upward direction.

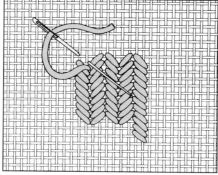

Slanting Satin Stitch
Each stitch spans two vertical and two horizontal canvas threads. Change the direction to produce different effects.

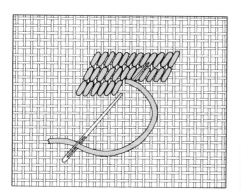

Gobelin Stitch
Work Gobelin stitch over one vertical and two horizontal threads. Slant the rows to left or right from one area to another.

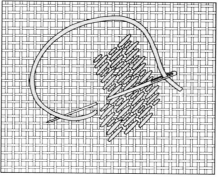

Cashmere Stitch
Work groups of three diagonal stitches to form steeply slanting rows, changing the direction from one area to another.

You will need:

The amount of canvas and threads you will need depends on the size of the chair seat you wish to cover. The finished embroidery for the chair shown measured 54cm (21¼in) along the front, 40cm (15¾in) along the back and 43cm (17in) along each side. The amounts given below will act as a guide for calculating your needs.

75cm×75cm (30in×30in) square of 10-gauge single thread canvas
Tapestry wool in the following colours and amounts: Blue grey: 12 skeins; mid grey: 10 skeins; light blue: 10 skeins; dull blue: 6 skeins; turquoise: 5 skeins; pink: 4 skeins; lavender: 5 skeins; rust: 3 skeins; orange: 3 skeins; dark rust: 1 skein; dark orange: 1 skein; and oddments of black, flesh pink, cream and green
Tapestry needle
75cm×75cm (30in×30in) square of hessian
Sewing thread and sewing needle
Rectangular embroidery frame
Small tacks and a hammer

To work the embroidery, first stretch the canvas in a rectangular frame, taking care to keep the canvas grain square. Then mark the outline of the area to be embroidered on to the canvas with tacking (basting) stitches. Do this by tacking the top and bottom edges first, then tack along the slanting side edges. Now find the centre of the canvas and mark with a few stitches.

Begin the embroidery by working the cat in tent stitch, starting at the marked centre of the canvas and working outwards. Follow the design from the chart,

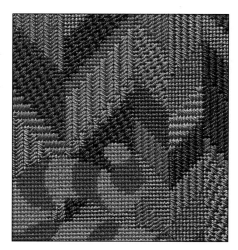

1 Remove the old seat covering from the chair. Trim the surplus canvas away, then lay your embroidery right side down on a clean, flat surface. Position the seat centrally over the canvas and fold up the edges of the canvas over the seat. Beginning at the midpoint of the top edge, tack the canvas securely in place.

2 Tack along the bottom and sides in the same way, pulling the canvas into shape and leaving the corners of the canvas free. At each corner, pull the canvas over the frame and insert a temporary tack. Check that you are happy with the fit at each corner and then hammer the tacks firmly home.

Above: Work the four stitches at random to fill the background shapes, using the colours indicated on the chart opposite.

Opposite: Follow the chart square by square, working from the centre outwards. Extend the colourful background so it will fit the seat shape by repeating the patterns.

3 Fold the two side pleats towards the tack and crease the canvas with your fingers. Cut away the top triangular section of each pleat, cutting along the fold line as shown. Then, to neaten each corner, fold over the remaining side flaps and secure with a temporary tack. Adjust if necessary, then hammer in the tack.

4 Trim away the canvas to within 1cm (½in) of the tacks. Tack the hessian to the frame, turning under the raw edges and folding the corners neatly. Replace the covered seat in the chair frame, inserting the back edge first. Push the seat well down into the frame, tapping it in place using a hammer wrapped in thick cloth.

remembering that each coloured square on the chart represents one vertical and one horizontal canvas thread.

Next, work the background in grey, blue, turquoise, pink and lavender. Use all four stitches shown on page 30, repeating them at random as shown in the close-up photograph above. Extend the background by repeating the shapes until the embroidery has reached the required size. To finish, add the mouth, claws and whiskers using back stitch (see page 36).

Blocking the Canvas
Remove the canvas from the frame, then block it to straighten out the embroidery. Spray with plain water, then tack down on to a board covered with polythene using rust-proof tacks. Pull the embroidery into shape as you proceed, then spray again and leave at room temperature until dry. Finally, cover the chair seat with your canvaswork by following steps one to four (left).

SWEET SCENTED CUSHION

Pure silk, twenty different shades of thread and a delightful summery grey cat combine to make a tiny cushion with the delicious fragrance of roses. This challenging project provides the perfect opportunity for you to show off your skills with needle and thread.

Trace off the pattern from page 37 and transfer it on to a square of raw silk, 30cm×30cm (12in×12in), using dressmakers' carbon paper. Tack (baste) the silk on to the backing fabric and stretch it in an embroidery hoop.

Using the colours shown on the pattern, work the embroidery in three strands of thread throughout. Six different stitches have been used to work this design and these are all described in detail overleaf. First, work the large flowers and leaves in satin stitch, then the stems and stamens in back stitch. Next, work the grey parts of the cat in long and short stitch, mixing two shades of grey. Use rows of running stitch to work the white areas and the whiskers,

satin stitch for the eyes and the tip of the nose, and back stitch for the mouth and nose outlines. Work the butterfly in satin stitch and straight stitch.

Next, work the central area of the foreground in straight stitch, keeping the stitches upright. Using the close-up photographs as a stitch guide, work the right-hand section of the foreground using rows of satin stitch, random straight stitch, rows of back stitch and French knots. Work the left-hand side using random straight stitch and blocks of satin stitch set at varying angles.

When the embroidery is complete, remove the hoop and press the silk lightly on the wrong side, taking care not to flatten the stitching.

Making Up the Cushion

The finished cushion measures 19cm (7½in) square. When you trim the embroidered silk you must allow a 1cm (½in) seam allowance all round, therefore making it 21cm (8½in) square.

Make up a length of piping (see page 28) from the strip of silk. With right sides together, tack (baste) the piping round the embroidery, making small snips at the corners, then sew it in place. Place the back cushion piece against the front, right sides together, then pin, tack and sew close to the piping, leaving an opening in one side. Clip the corners and turn the cover the right way out. Fill with stuffing mixed with pot pourri, then slip stitch the opening closed.

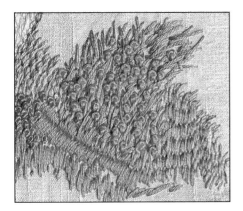

Mix different turquoise and green threads together in the needle to work the foliage. French knots add texture and interest to the surface.

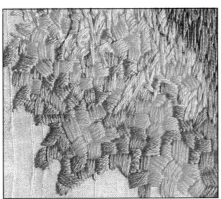

Work some areas of foliage in pale green random straight stitch. Other areas can be worked in blocks of satin stitch set at varying angles.

35

EMBROIDERY STITCHES

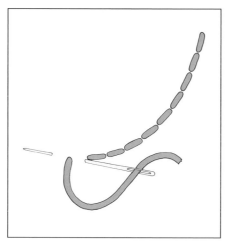

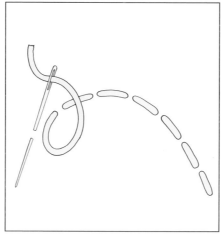

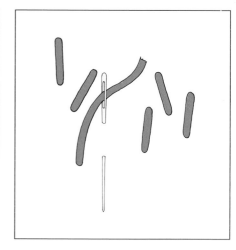

Back Stitch

Work back stitch with a forward and backward motion, as shown, keeping the stitches small and even. The finished result should give a fine, neat line rather like machine stitching.

Running Stitch

Running stitch is very simple to work by passing the needle and thread in and out of the fabric at regular intervals, as shown. Use this stitch for working lines and also in rows to fill a shape.

Straight Stitch

Simple to work, straight stitch makes an effective filling. Work all the stitches in the same direction, or with varying slants so the stitches cross at random to give a less formal effect.

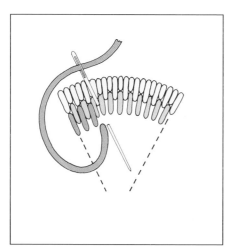

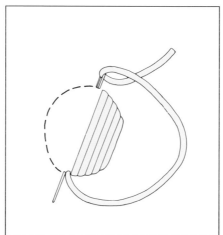

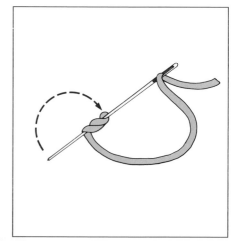

Long and Short Stitch

Begin by working a row of alternately long and short stitches following the outline of the shape. Work the subsequent rows using stitches of equal length. No fabric should show through the stitching.

Satin Stitch

Satin stitch needs to be worked evenly to avoid puckering the fabric. Work straight stitches side by side to fill the shape, arranging them close together so they completely cover the fabric.

French Knot

Hold the thread taut on the surface with your left hand, twisting the needle around it two or three times. Tighten the twists, turn the needle and insert it back into the fabric. Pull the needle through.

Here is your full size pattern for the scented cushion. Trace it directly from the page and use dressmakers' carbon paper to transfer it on to your silk square.

LITERARY CATS

Alphabets and numerals have long been a feature of sampler designs and they are always a popular subject to embroider. This modern alphabet sampler is decorated with grey, black, tortoiseshell and tabby cats sitting in a line, obviously intent on learning their letters.

The embroidery in this sampler is worked mainly in cross stitch, with sections of the cats outlined in Holbein stitch. Both stitches are very easy to work and, as you are using fabric with a weave which can be counted to keep the stitches even, the finished picture will be neatly executed.

Begin by neatening the edges of the fabric to prevent them from fraying. Do this by turning a double 1cm (½in) hem all the way round, tacking (basting) it in position. Alternatively, use a row of large machine zig-zag stitches to cover the raw edges. Run a vertical and horizontal line of tacking stitches across the fabric so the lines cross at the centre point. Stretch the fabric in the embroidery hoop, keeping the fabric grain straight and moving the hoop as necessary. If you prefer, you can work the fabric mounted in a rectangular frame or stretcher rather than a hoop.

Working the Embroidery

First, find the centre square on the chart on page 40 and then, starting from the corresponding point on your fabric, begin to stitch the red and blue alphabet, following the coloured squares on the chart. Work outwards from the centre and use three strands of thread for all the embroidery. Remember that each square on the chart represents one woven block of fabric.

When the alphabet is complete, work the row of turquoise and purple numerals, beginning at the centre of the row. Take care to line up the numerals in the correct position underneath the letters on the last row of the alphabet.

Work the main portion of the striped border next, beginning at the centre top and continuing downwards until you reach the point where the cats are lined up along the base. Then stitch the isolated geometric designs above and below the alphabet, again checking the spacing carefully. Return to the border and work the solid areas of the cats, continuing the striped border across the spaces in between. Outline the white areas of the tortoiseshell cats in black thread using Holbein stitch.

When the whole design has been stitched, remove it from the hoop and press the embroidery on the wrong side over a well-padded surface, taking care not to flatten the stitching. For best results, have your sampler framed professionally, laced over a sheet of strong cardboard (or hardboard).

EMBROIDERY STITCHES

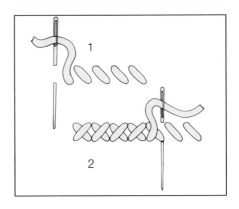

Cross Stitch

Work cross stitch in rows on even-weave fabric to give a neat finish. First, work a row of diagonal stitches (1) from right to left of the shape being covered. Then work the top diagonals as shown in 2, moving in the opposite direction.

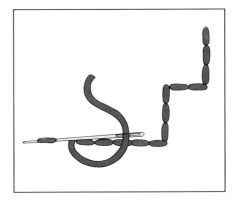

Holbein Stitch

Holbein stitch is ideal for working outlines on even-weave fabric. First, work a row of evenly spaced stitches along the edge of the shape, stepping the row where necessary. Fill in the spaces by working back in the opposite direction.

PINK APPLIQUÉ SWEATSHIRT

*B*righten up a plain cotton sweatshirt by adding a stylized cat motif. To solve the problem of embroidering directly on to a ready-made garment, work the cat on a background fabric first, then cut it out and stitch it to the sweatshirt. The original design was made in pink and lavender, but the cat would look equally stunning worked in a bright, primary colour against a black or dark blue background.

You will need:
Pink cotton sweatshirt
25cm×25cm (10in×10in) square of lavender cotton fabric
25cm×25cm (10in×10in) square of tear-off backing for embroidery (e.g. 'Stitch 'n' Tear')
40cm×40cm (16in×16in) square of thin white cotton backing fabric
1 skein of stranded cotton thread in lavender, plus oddments of black, grey, white, turquoise and pink
Packet of bonding web
Crewel needle
Sewing needle and lavender thread
Tracing paper and pencil
Dressmakers' carbon paper
Large embroidery hoop
Pair of small, sharp scissors

One square represents 12mm (½in)

First, carefully copy the pattern shown left on to a grid, enlarging it to the required size by following the instructions on page 7. Each square of your grid should measure 12mm sq (½in sq).

Transfer the enlarged pattern on to the right side of the lavender fabric using dressmakers' carbon paper and a sharp pencil. Lay the fabric face down on an ironing board, then cover with a slightly smaller piece of bonding web, web side down, and press firmly with a dry iron to bond the two fabrics together. Allow the fabrics to cool.

Next, following the outline marked on the lavender fabric, carefully cut out the cat using a pair of small sharp scissors. Peel off the paper backing from the bonding web, then place the cat face up on the white backing fabric, positioning it in the centre. Cover with a damp cloth and press carefully to bond the two pieces of fabric together. Position the piece of tear-off backing underneath the

41

EMBROIDERY STITCHES

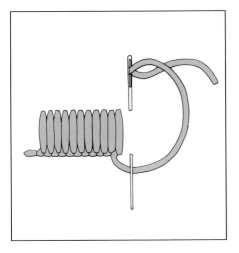

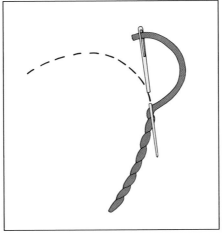

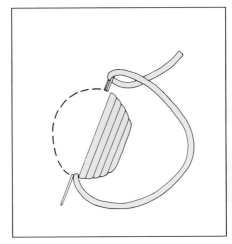

Buttonhole Stitch
Work buttonhole stitch from left to right over the raw edge. Pull the needle through the fabric and over the thread, as shown, to create a row of upright stitches linked by a looped edge.

Stem Stitch
Work stem stitch with a forward and backward movement, as shown, keeping the stitches evenly worked and of the same size. Always keep the working thread to the right of the needle.

Satin Stitch
Satin stitch needs to be worked evenly to avoid puckering the fabric. Work straight stitches side by side to fill the shape, arranging them close together so they completely cover the fabric.

Work a row of buttonhole stitch round the cat shape, taking the stitches right over the raw edge and into the backing fabric. Make the stitches about 6mm (¼in) long and work them evenly and closely together so that the fabric does not show through.

backing fabric and tack (baste) the fabrics together, following the cat outline closely. Now mount the design in a large embroidery hoop.

Stitch the outline of the cat first. Use three strands of lavender stranded cotton thread and buttonhole stitch (see above), taking the stitches right over the raw edge of the lavender fabric into the backing fabric. Make the stitches about 6mm (¼in) long and work them evenly and closely together so that no fabric shows between.

Next, embroider the inside of the legs and the claws using stem stitch and the same coloured thread. Finally, embroider the features, using three strands of thread in the colours indicated on the pattern. (Keep in mind that the whiskers cannot be completed until the cat has been sewn on to the sweatshirt.) Work the eyes in satin stitch, then outline the eyes with back stitch (see page 36).

Work the mouth in stem stitch and the nose in satin stitch. Work pink French knots (see page 36) scattered randomly around the nose, then work the whiskers in stem stitch, stopping 1cm (½in) from the edge of the cat.

Attaching the Design
Remove the hoop and carefully pull away the tear-off backing from round the embroidery on the reverse of the fabric. Press the embroidery lightly on the wrong side over a well-padded surface, taking care not to crush the stitches. Cut the backing fabric away from round the cat. Then use a small sharp pair of scissors to cut close around the buttonhole stitching. Position the cat on the front of the sweatshirt and pin it in place. Using matching sewing thread, slip stitch the cat securely to the sweatshirt. Complete the whiskers in stem stitch, carrying the stitching on to the sweatshirt.

TINY TOTS ROMPER SUIT

Knit a cheerful, brightly-coloured romper suit for an active toddler. Quick and easy to knit in stocking stitch and rib, the front of the suit features an attractive cat motif worked in Swiss darning. Obviously, an experienced knitter could knit the design if preferred.

Sizes

To fit 66[71]cm (26[28]in) chest.

Tension

24 sts and 29 rows to 10cm (4in) on 4mm (6) needles over stocking stitch.

Abbreviations

Knitting abbreviations are given on page 64.

Sweater – back

Using 3¾mm (5) needles and A, cast on 74[80] sts and work in K1, P1 rib for 3[3]cm (1¼[1¼]in).
Change to 4mm (6) needles and B and work straight in st st until the back measures 24[26]cm (9½[10¼]in) from cast-on edge, ending with a WS row.
Cast off 7[7] sts at the beg of the next two rows.
60[66] sts. **
Cont straight until back measures 38[41]cm (15[16]in) from cast-on edge, ending with a WS row.

Shape back neck

Next row K17[19] sts, turn and work on this set of sts only.
*** Change to A and work two rows straight in st st.
Without breaking off yarn, place these sts on a stitch holder. Place centre 26[28] sts on a stitch holder.
With RS facing, rejoin yarn B to rem sts and work to end of row.
Work as for first side from *** to end.

You will need:

Approximately 175[200]g (7[8]oz) of lightweight double knitting wool in main colour, A (blue)
Approximately 150[175]g (6[7]oz) of the same yarn in contrast colour, B (yellow)
Oddments of the same yarn in white, black and green for embroidery
1 pair each of 3¾mm (US size 5) and 4mm (US size 6) needles
6 stitch holders or spare needles
6 yellow buttons
Tapestry needle
1cm- (½in-) wide elastic for waist

Sweater – front

Work as for back to **.
60[66] sts.
Cont straight until front measures 30.5[33.5]cm (12[13]in) from cast-on edge, ending with a WS row.

Shape front neck

Next row K25[28] sts, turn and work

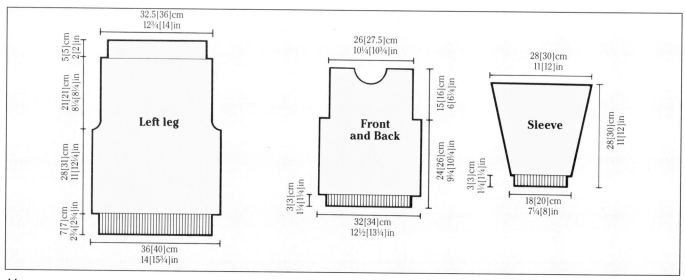

Left leg — 32.5[36]cm 12¾[14]in; 5[5]cm 2[2]in; 21[21]cm 8¼[8¼]in; 28[31]cm 11[12¼]in; 7[7]cm 2¾[2¾]in; 36[40]cm 14[15¾]in

Front and Back — 26[27.5]cm 10¼[10¾]in; 15[16]cm 6[6¼]in; 24[26]cm 9¼[10¼]in; 3[3]cm 1¼[1¼]in; 32[34]cm 12½[13¼]in

Sleeve — 28[30]cm 11[12]in; 28[30]cm 11[12]in; 3[3]cm 1¼[1¼]in; 18[20]cm 7¼[8]in

on this set of sts only.
**** Work one row.
Then, dec 1 st at neck edge on next row and every foll alt row until 17[19] sts remain.
Work a few rows straight until front measures 5mm (¼in) less than back to shoulder.
Change to A and work two rows st st.
Without breaking off yarn, place these sts on a stitch holder.
Place centre 10[10] sts on a stitch holder.
With RS facing, rejoin yarn to rem sts and work to end of row.
Now work as for first side from **** to end.

Sleeves (make 2)

Using 3¾mm (5) needles and A, cast on 44[48] sts and work in K1, P1 rib for 3[3]cm (1¼[1¼]in).
Change to 4mm (6) needles and work in st st and A, **at the same time**, inc 1 st at each end of next and every foll 4th row until there are 66[72] sts on the needle.
Cont straight in st st until sleeve measures 28[30]cm (11[12]in) from cast-on edge, ending with a WS row.
Cast off loosely.

Back left shoulder band

With RS facing, 3¾mm (5) needles and A, pick up and K17[19] sts from stitch holder.
Work seven rows in K1, P1 rib.
Cast off loosely in rib.

Back right shoulder band

Work in the same way as for back left shoulder band.

Back neckband

With RS facing, 3¾mm (5) needles and A, pick up and knit 8[8] sts from left shoulder band, 2[2] sts down left side of neck, 26[28] sts from centre stitch holder, 2[2] sts up right side of neck and 8[8] sts from right shoulder band.
46[48] sts.

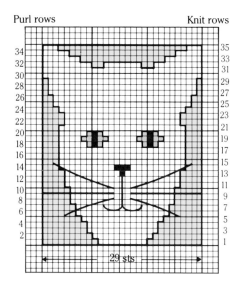

Purl rows   Knit rows

29 sts

Then work 7 rows in K1, P1 rib.
Cast off loosely in rib.

Front left shoulder band

With RS facing, 3¾mm (5) needles and
A, pick up and K17[19] sts from stitch
holder.
Work two rows in K1, P1 rib.
Now, work across the sts in rib, making
two evenly spaced buttonholes along
the row.
Work three more rows in rib, then cast
off loosely in rib.

Front right shoulder band

Work in the same way as for front left
shoulder band.

Front neckband

With RS facing, 3¾mm (5) needles and
A, pick up and knit 8[8] sts from left
shoulder band, 16[19] sts down left
side of neck, 10[10] sts from centre
stitch holder, 16[19] sts up right side of
neck and 8[8] sts from right shoulder
band.
58[64] sts.
Work two rows in K1, P1 rib.
Now, work across the sts in rib, making
one buttonhole at each end of the
neckband.

Work three more rows in rib, then cast
off loosely in rib.

To make up

Press each piece lightly on the wrong
side. Work the motif in Swiss darning,
following the chart (above) and
positioning it as shown in the
photograph on page 45. Use white for
the face, and black and green for the
eyes. Back stitch the mouth and
whiskers in black. Overlap the front
bands over the back bands and tack
(baste) together. With centre of sleeves
to shoulder, pin the sleeves in position
and stitch to the body. Remove tacking
and sew on three buttons at each side
of the bands to correspond with the
buttonholes.
Join side and sleeve seams.
Press all seams.

Trousers (make 2)

Using 3¾mm (5) needles and A, cast
on 76[82] sts and work in K1, P1 rib for
7[7]cm (2¾[2¾]in).
Increase row Work in st st, inc 12[14]
sts evenly across the row.
88[96] sts.
Change to 4mm (6) needles and B and

work 20 rows in st st.
Continue straight, working in alternate
twenty row stripes of A and B until leg
measures 28[31]cm (11[12¾]in) from
beg of rib.
Shape crotch
Cont in stripe patt, **at the same time**
dec 1 st at each end of next row and
every alt row until there are 78[86] sts
on the needle. Cont straight in patt
until work measures 49[52]cm
(19¼[20½]in) from beg of rib.
78[86] sts.
Decrease row Dec 12[14] sts evenly
across the next row.
Change to 3¾mm (5) needles and A
and work in K1, P1 rib for 5[5]cm
(2[2]in).
Cast off loosely in rib.

To make up

Press each piece lightly on the wrong
side. Join the front and back seams
and leg seam, reversing the seam at
the cuff. Turn back half of the waist
ribbing to the wrong side and sew
neatly in place, leaving an opening for
the elastic. Insert the elastic and
secure. Sew up the opening and turn
up the cuffs on the legs.

*Use a blunt-ended tapestry needle to work
Swiss darning. Start at the base of the
motif and work from right to left, making
each stitch in two stages, as shown. Turn
the work at the end of each row.*

*To ring the changes, use a different colour
scheme and vary the cat motifs. Here,
bright turquoise and rust are used to make
a plain suit with cat motifs embroidered
on the legs and sleeves.*

SNUGGLEPUSS SWEATER

*R*ows of black cats on a boldly striped background make a stunning design for this colourful kid's sweater. Knit the design in stocking stitch, following the chart square by square, and strand the yarn not in use loosely across the back of the work.

The pattern for this charming child's sweater gives you a choice of three sizes. And it can always be knitted in a heavier yarn to fit an adult.

You will need:

4[5:5] 25 g (1oz) balls of 4 ply shetland
  wool in main colour, A (green)
3[3:4] 25g (1oz) balls of the same yarn
  in contrast colour, B (purple)
3[3:4] 25g (1oz) balls of the same yarn
  in contrast colour, C (black)
1 pair each of 2¾mm (US size 1) and
  3¼mm (US size 3) needles
2 stitch holders

Sizes

To fit 61[66:71]cm (24[26:28]in) chest.

Tension

28 sts and 34 rows to 10cm (4in) on
3¼mm (3) needles over pattern.

Abbreviations

Knitting abbreviations are given on
page 64.

Back

Using 2¾mm (1) needles and A, cast
on 96[100:104] sts and work in K2, P2
rib for 4.5cm (1¾in).
Change to 3¼mm (3) needles and
work in st st from chart, reading knit
rows (odd numbered rows) from right
to left and purl rows (even numbered
rows) from left to right.
1st size Repeat the 24 stitch patt 4
times across the row.
2nd and 3rd sizes Work the edge
stitches at each side of the 4 repeats as
indicated on the chart.
Cont to repeat the 40 rows of chart
until the back measures
26.5[27.5:28.5]cm
(10½[10¾:11]in) from cast-on edge,
ending with a WS row.
Mark each end of next row with
contrast yarn to denote beg of
armholes.**
Cont straight working from chart until
back measures 41[42:43]cm
(16½[17¼:18]in) from cast-on edge,
ending with a WS row.

Shape back neck

Next row Patt 31[33:35] sts, turn and
work on this set of sts only.
*** Patt 1 row.
Keeping patt correct, dec 1 st at neck
edge on next 3 rows. 28[30:32] sts.
Work 1 row.
Cast off loosely.
Place centre 34 sts on a stitch holder.
With RS facing, rejoin yarn to rem sts
and patt to end of row.
Now work as for first side from *** to
end.

Front

Work as for back to **.
Cont to rep the 40 rows of chart patt
until front measures 37[38:39]cm
(14¼[15¼:15¾]in) from cast-on edge,
ending with a WS row.

Shape front neck

Next row Patt 39[41:43] sts, turn and
work on this set of sts only.
**** Patt 1 row.
Keeping patt correct, dec 1 st at neck
edge on next row and foll 6 rows, and
then at neck edge on every foll alt row
until 28[30:32] sts remain.
Break off B and C and cont in st st and
A. Work a few rows straight until front
measures the same as back to
shoulder.
Cast off loosely.
Place centre 18 sts on a stitch holder.
With RS facing, rejoin yarn to rem sts
and patt to end of row.
Now work as for first side from **** to
end.

Sleeves

Using 2¾mm (1) needles and A, cast
on 52[56:60] sts and work in K2, P2 rib

*Knit your Snugglepuss Sweater in stocking
stitch, following the design on the chart
(right) square by square. Repeat the cat
designs every 40 rows, but continue to
work the stripes in sequence. The
photograph (top right) shows a detail of
the completed design.*

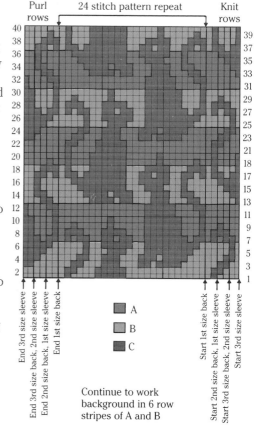

Purl rows   24 stitch pattern repeat   Knit rows

End 3rd size back, 2nd size sleeve
End 3rd size back, 2nd size sleeve
End 2nd size back, 1st size sleeve
End 1st size back

Start 1st size back
Start 2nd size back, 1st size sleeve
Start 3rd size back, 2nd size sleeve
Start 3rd size sleeve

☐ A
☐ B
■ C

Continue to work
background in 6 row
stripes of A and B

for 4.5cm (1¾in).
Change to 3¼mm (3) needles and work in st st from chart, working the edge stitches for 1st, 2nd and 3rd sizes as indicated on first row (knit row) of chart.
The first row sets the patt.
Cont in patt as set, **at the same time**, inc 1 st at each end of next and every foll 4th row until 96[100:104] sts are on the needle, working inc sts into patt.
Cont straight in patt until sleeve measures 37[39:41]cm (14¼[15¾:16½]in) from cast-on edge, ending with a WS row.
Break off B and C and cont straight in st st and A until sleeve measures 39[41:43]cm (15¾[16½:18]in) from cast-on edge. Cast off loosely.

Neckband

Join right shoulder seam.
Using 2¾mm (1) needles, A and with RS facing, pick up and knit 26[28:30] sts down left side of front neck, K18 sts on holder, pick up and knit 26[28:30] sts up right side of front neck, K7[7:7] sts along back neck, K34 sts from holder, pick up and knit 7[7:7] sts along other side of back neck. 118[122:126] sts.

Next row K2, *P2, K2, rep from * to end.
Next row P2, *K2, P2, rep from * to end.
Rep last 2 rows until 10 rib rows have been worked in all.
Cast off loosely in rib.

To make up

Press each piece lightly on the wrong side.
Join the left shoulder and neckband seam.
With centre of sleeves to shoulder, pin the sleeves in position between the coloured markers and stitch to the body.
Join the side and sleeve seams.
Press all seams.

The two samples show how easy it is to create alternative effects from a chart by simply changing the colours. Knit the cat motifs in two shades of orange, grey or brown to make tabby cats (above right) or contrast black or white cats against a brightly coloured background (right). Alternatively, you can create different effects by changing the depth of the background stripes, working them either two, four or eight rows deep.

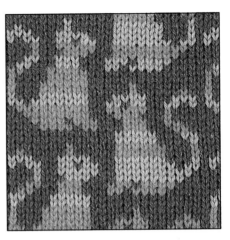

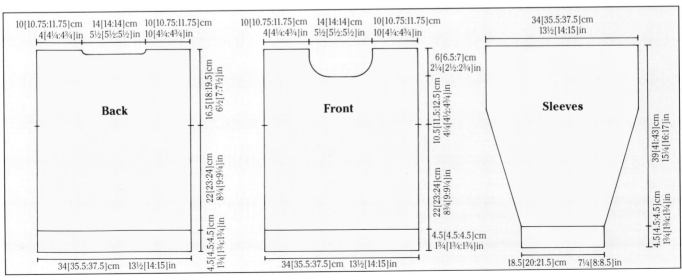

CUDDLY KITTEN

This cuddly toy kitten will delight any child and, providing you follow the instructions carefully, you should not find it too difficult to make. To achieve the best results, always use good quality fabrics and fillings, but, for safety reasons, don't add the whiskers if you are making the toy for a very young child.

You will need:

25cm (¼yd) of short grey fur
Small piece of short white fur
Plastic whiskers (optional)
13mm (½in) pink plastic nose
Pair of 15mm (⅝in) safety eyes with washers
Pink embroidery thread
Dacron and polyester filling

Enlarge the pattern overleaf as described on page 7. Each square of your grid should measure 2.5cm (1in). Now trace the pattern pieces on to cardboard and cut them out, being sure to mark important points such as the eye position, darts and slits. Also mark the direction of pile carefully; this is indicated by an arrow on each pattern piece.

Mark an arrow on the reverse of your fur fabrics to indicate the direction of pile, then position the pattern templates accordingly. Draw round the outlines with a felt-tip pen and cut the pieces out. If two asymmetrical pieces are required, turn the template over before drawing the second one (without changing direction of pile) to get a mirror image of the first piece.

Now follow steps one to six to make up the toy. For the best results, always pin then tack (baste) a seam before you sew it. Other handy tips on toymaking are given in the box right.

USEFUL STITCHES

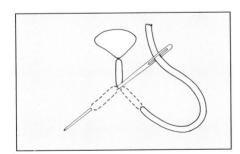

To sew the mouth, push the needle through from the base of the head to the tip of the nose. Sew three small stitches as shown above to form a Y shape.

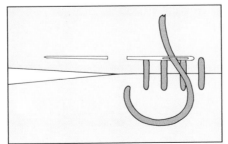

Ladder stitch (above) is used for closing gaps in seams and for attaching the head to the body. Pull the stitches tight as you go so that they are barely visible.

TOYMAKING TIPS

Always choose good quality fur fabrics.

Beginners should choose fur fabrics with a knitted backing; they stretch slightly and do not fray, making them easier to work with.

When positioning pattern templates on fabric, pay special attention to arrows indicating direction of pile.

Cut fur pieces out of single thickness fabric only.

Reverse the pattern template when cutting a second asymmetrical piece out of fur.

Always pin then tack (baste) a seam before you sew it by machine or hand.

Pin fur fabrics with glass headed pins as they are easier to find; pins left in toys cause a serious danger to children.

Sew fabric pieces together with right sides facing unless stated otherwise.

Use a strong sewing thread for sewing seams; one containing man-made fibres is best as it will stretch slightly.

Use a teasel brush to pull out fur trapped in seams.

Use a long blunt instrument such as a thick knitting needle or a Phillips screwdriver to help you turn your toy.

Sew heads on with ladder stitch, using strong button thread and a large darning needle; sew round at least twice to secure firmly.

Always use good quality filling – old stockings and scraps of fabric give a poor finished look to your toy.

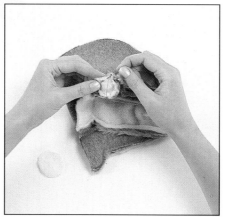

1 With the fabrics placed right sides together, sew the white linings to the ear pieces, leaving the straight edge open. Turn the ears the right way out and machine top stitch close to the seams so that the ears are flattened. On one side head piece, gather the upper edge of the slit to the point marked X and then sew the slit closed. Repeat on the other side.

2 Using a pair of small, sharp-pointed scissors, cut slits for the ears as marked, then place the two side heads right sides together and sew seam H-J. Ease the head gusset into position between points H and K on one side head piece. Sew in place and repeat on the other side. Pierce tiny holes at the eye positions and at H for the nose.

3 From inside the head, push the ears into the slits so that the raw edges are together. Sew into place. Turn the head the right way out and insert the eyes and nose, securing with the safety washers. Also insert the whiskers at this point. Stuff the head carefully, moulding the shape as you go, then gather the raw edge with running stitch to close the gap.

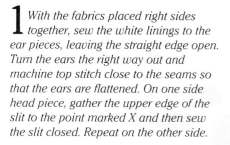

4 Sew the mouth with pink embroidery thread as shown on page 51, then lay the head to one side. Close the dart on the front body and attach the inside legs to either side between points A and B. Sew the side body pieces on to the inside legs between points A and C. Then sew seam D-E on either side, between the front and rear paws.

5 Open out the base of one front leg and, with right sides together, ease a paw pad into position. Sew the pad in place and repeat for the other leg. Close seam F-G along the back of the body. Fold the tail in half and sew from the tip to the base. Turn the right way out and tack (baste), with right sides together, on to the under body at G.

6 Open out the base of the main body and ease the base body into position, matching points G and E and tucking the tail inside. Sew in place, turn the body the right way out and stuff it firmly. Make sure the body sits correctly, then close the neck by gathering it with running stitch. Finally, sew the head in position using ladder stitch.

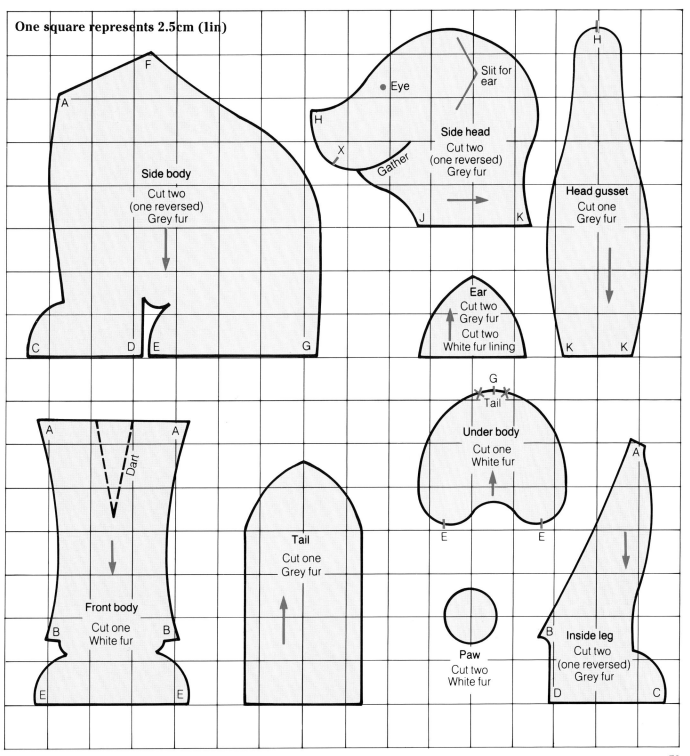

One square represents 2.5cm (1in)

F
A

Side body
Cut two
(one reversed)
Grey fur

C   D E   G

● Eye

Slit for
ear

H

X

Gather

Side head
Cut two
(one reversed)
Grey fur

J   K

H

Head gusset
Cut one
Grey fur

K   K

Ear
Cut two
Grey fur
Cut two
White fur lining

G
Tail

Under body
Cut one
White fur

E   E

A   A

Dart

Front body
Cut one
White fur

B   B

E   E

Tail
Cut one
Grey fur

Paw
Cut two
White fur

A

B **Inside leg**
Cut two
(one reversed)
Grey fur

D   C

PURRFECT PURSE

*T*he purrfect gift for any little girl, this delightful toy has a secret pocket in the back for storing special possessions. Make it in bold black and white fur fabric and attach a length of brightly coloured cord to hang around the child's neck.

Draw the pattern on pages 56/57 to the full size as described on page 7. Be sure to complete the pocket lining pattern piece by reversing the image along the dotted line. Cut out the paper pattern pieces and make templates of them by tracing them on to cardboard. Cut these out also.

Mark the position of the dart, eye, tail and so on, and draw arrows on each piece to indicate the direction of pile. Mark the direction of pile on the reverse of your fur fabrics then lay your templates down accordingly. Trace round the outlines with a felt-tip pen, repeating the procedure where more than one piece is required. Cut out all the pieces, then follow steps one to eight to make up the toy.

You will need:
30cm (⅜yd) of short black fur
Small piece of short white fur
35cm×20cm (14in×7in) piece of
    black velvet lining
15mm (⅝in) pink plastic nose
Pair of 15mm (⅝in) safety eyes with
    washers
Pink embroidery thread
Small button
Short piece 5mm- (½in-) wide elastic
Length of red cord
Dacron and polyester filling

1 First sew the white ear linings to the two front head pieces between points C and D. Then close the darts. Place the two front head pieces together with right sides facing and sew between points E and F. Now, with right sides facing, attach the back head to the face, matching points E and F, and sewing all the way round the outline as shown above.

2 Cut a slit in the back of the head (in the position marked on the pattern) and pierce tiny holes for the eyes and nose. Turn the head the right way out through the slit. Flatten the ears and machine top stitch across their base, through all layers. Insert the eyes and nose, securing on the reverse with the washers, then stuff the head firmly.

3 Embroider the mouth with pink embroidery thread, referring to the diagram on page 51. Then lay the head to one side. Sew the paw pieces to the arms along A-B as shown, keeping right sides together. Now fold the arms in half and sew round the outline, leaving the straight bottom edge open. Turn the right way out and fill lightly with stuffing.

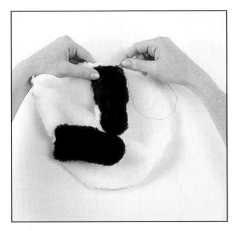

4 Fold the leg pieces in half and sew around the side seam, leaving the straight bottom edge open. Repeat for the tail, then turn all three pieces out the right way. Place a little stuffing into each leg. Now place the two front body pieces right sides together and sew seam G-H. Tack the arms into position on the front body as shown and repeat with the legs.

5 Cut a slit in the pocket lining fabric at the position indicated on the pattern. Fold a 5cm (2in) piece of 5mm- (¼in-) wide black elastic in half and tack (baste) it into position against the slit, raw edges together, on the right side of the fabric. Place the lining on to the back body piece, right sides together, and sew a line of stitching all around the slit as shown.

6 Using a pair of small, sharp-pointed scissors, cut the slit right through the fur fabric, then snip diagonally into the stitched corners at either end of the slit, being careful not to cut the stitching. Push the lining through the slit on to the reverse side and flatten out. Now fold the lining in half and sew around the three raw edges as shown to form a pocket.

through all thicknesses. Place the two body pieces right sides together, with the limbs well tucked in, and sew round the outline, leaving a gap for turning. Turn the body the right way out and lightly fill the neck and stomach. Sew the gap closed with ladder stitch.

8 Push the neck of the body through the slit on the back of the head and ladder stitch firmly in place. Then sew a button opposite the elastic loop on the pocket. Take a length of thick red cord and tie a knot 2cm (¾in) from each end. Place one end of the cord across a paw as shown then fold the paw over and sew it to the arm so that the knot of the cord is trapped. Tuck the cord end up into the paw

7 Cut a slit in the back body for the tail and, with right sides facing, insert the tail into the opening so that raw edges are together. Sew firmly in place, as shown,

and repeat for the other side, adjusting the length of cord to suit the size of the child. Finish off with a bright red bow to match the colour of the cord.

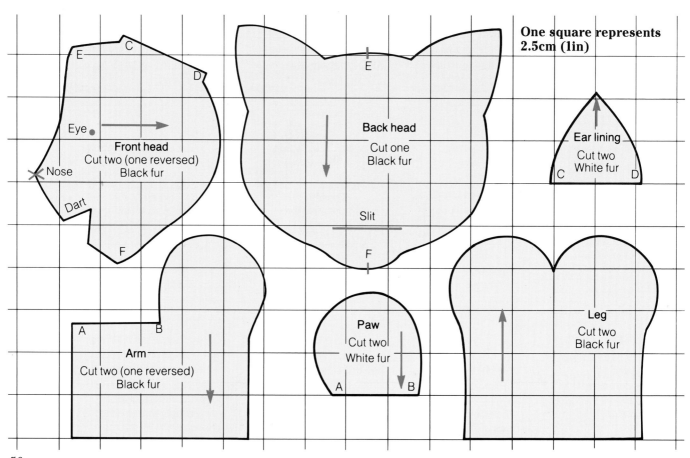

One square represents 2.5cm (1in)

E — C
D

Eye •
Front head
Cut two (one reversed)
Black fur

× Nose

Dart

F

E

Back head
Cut one
Black fur

Slit

F

Ear lining
Cut two
White fur
C   D

A   B
Arm
Cut two (one reversed)
Black fur

Paw
Cut two
White fur
A   B

Leg
Cut two
Black fur

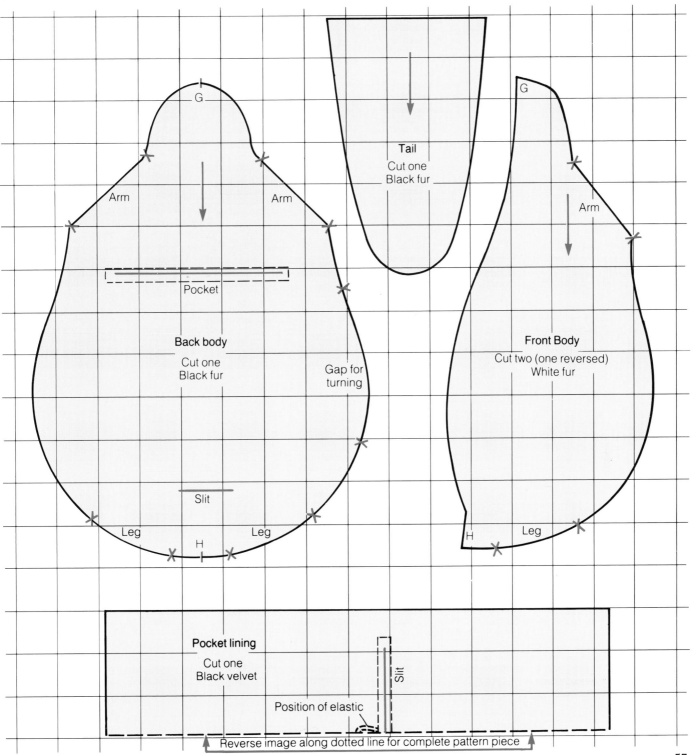

Tail
Cut one
Black fur

Back body
Cut one
Black fur

G

Arm

Arm

Pocket

Gap for
turning

Slit

Leg

H

Leg

Front Body
Cut two (one reversed)
White fur

G

Arm

H

Leg

Pocket lining
Cut one
Black velvet

Slit

Position of elastic

Reverse image along dotted line for complete pattern piece

PERSIAN NIGHTIE CASE

Adorn your bed with this adorable Persian cat – and provide the perfect place for your nightdress at the same time. Cut out the long fur fabric with a pair of small, sharp-pointed scissors, carefully snipping the back of the fabric without cutting through the pile of the fur.

You will need:
½m (½yd) of long white fur fabric
60cm×60cm (24in×24in) square of short white fur
50cm×50cm (20in×20in) square of white brushed cotton lining fabric
15mm pink plastic nose
Pair 18mm safety eyes with washers
Pink embroidery thread
Small button
Short piece 5mm- (¼in-) wide elastic
Dacron and polyester filling

This is quite a complex design so, if you are new to soft toymaking, it might be advisable to gain a little experience before tackling it by making the Cuddly Kitten or the Purrfect Purse first. You will find some useful tips on soft toymaking on page 51, so read these carefully before you begin.

Draw the pattern pieces on to a 2.5cm sq (1in sq) grid and cut them out. Trace round them on to cardboard to make templates and mark the position of the eyes, ears, darts and so forth, paying particular attention to the arrows indicating direction of pile. Note that the lining and tail pattern must be reversed along the dotted line to give the full pattern piece.

Choose good quality fur fabrics for the nightie case as these will give you the best results. Mark an arrow on the back of the fabrics to show the direction of pile and position the templates accordingly. Trace round the outlines, reversing the template if a second asymmetrical piece is required. Now carefully cut out all the pieces.

Follow steps one to nine to make up the case, then use a teasel brush to pull out any long fur trapped in the seams.

1 *Close the darts on both of the front side face pieces then sew the slit closed as shown. Place the two face pieces right sides together and sew seam S-T. Now sew the nose gusset into place, matching points W-S-W. Next sew the linings to the fur ear pieces, leaving the straight bottom edges open. Turn the right way out and machine top stitch close to the edge.*

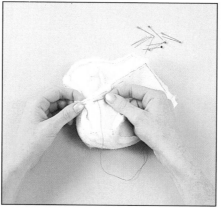

2 *Sew the two side head pieces on to the head gusset between W and Y. Cut slits in the side heads as marked and insert the ears, with linings facing forward and raw edges together. Sew in place. Matching points Z and W on either side, sew the side head to the front face as shown. Pierce tiny holes for the eyes and turn the head the right way out.*

3 *Push the eye stalks through the felt backing pieces and insert the eyes into the head. Secure on the back with safety washers, then insert the nose and secure in the same way. Stuff the head gently, moulding the front face by adding extra filling to the cheeks, then close the gap with a line of running stitch gathered tightly around the opening.*

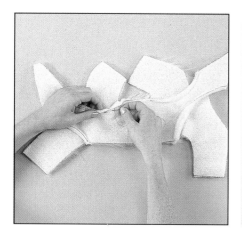

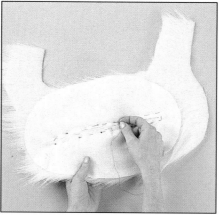

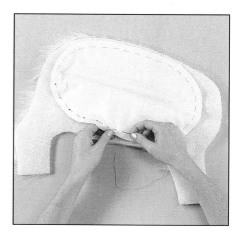

4 *Embroider the mouth with pink embroidery thread, referring to the diagram on page 51. Then put the head to one side. Join the four leg pieces to the body gusset, making sure that all the letters marked on the pattern are teamed correctly. Fold the tail in half and sew along the side seam, leaving the straight bottom edge open. Turn the right way out.*

5 *Cut a slit, as marked on the pattern, in one of the lining fabric pieces. Fold a 5cm (2in) piece of 5mm- (¼in-) wide white elastic in half and tack (baste) it in position against the slit, on the right side of the fabric. Place the lining on to the base body piece with right sides together, then sew a line of stitching all around the slit as shown above.*

6 *With a pair of sharp-pointed scissors, cut the slit right through the fur fabric, then snip diagonally into the stitched corners at either end of the slit, being careful not to cut the stitching. Push the lining through the slit on to the reverse side and flatten out. Place the other lining piece on top and sew the two lining pieces together as shown.*

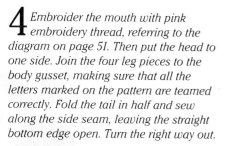

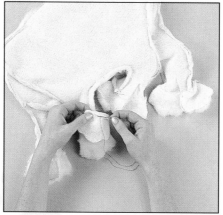

7 *With right sides together, join the body gusset to the base body between X and O. Then sew seams P-Q and R-N. Place the top body over the base body and join seams X-J, K-L and M-N as shown. Finally, sew seam X-N along the back of the body, leaving a gap for turning and inserting the tail into the seam at the point indicated on the pattern.*

8 *Cut slits in the base of the legs at the positions marked on the pattern. Open out the base of each leg and sew a paw piece to either side along the straight edge as shown. Place each pair of paws right sides together and sew from the beginning of one slit right round the paw to the end of the other slit, tapering the seam to a point at either end.*

9 *Turn the body the right way out and fill softly with lightweight stuffing, ensuring that the lining bag remains flat. Then close the gap with a ladder stitch. Position the head on the body and ladder stitch firmly in place using strong thread. Finally, sew a button on to the base of the body, opposite the elastic loop. A satin bow completes the picture.*

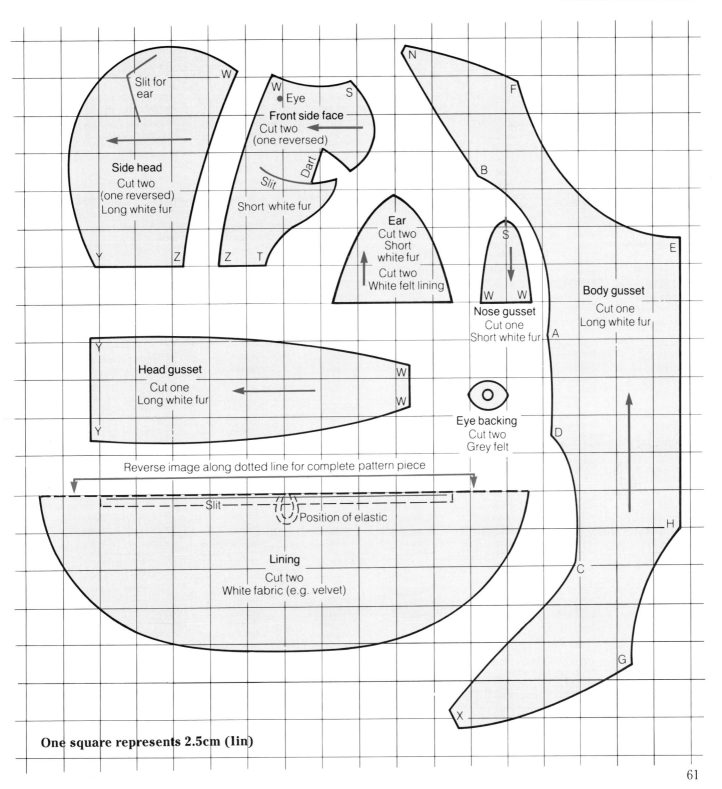

Slit for ear

W

Side head
Cut two
(one reversed)
Long white fur

Y   Z

W   S
● Eye
Front side face
Cut two
(one reversed)

Dart

Slit

Z   T

Short white fur

Ear
Cut two
Short
white fur
Cut two
White felt lining

N

F

B

S

W   W

Nose gusset
Cut one
Short white fur

E

Body gusset
Cut one
Long white fur

A

Y   W

Head gusset
Cut one
Long white fur

W

Y

Eye backing
Cut two
Grey felt

D

Reverse image along dotted line for complete pattern piece

Slit   Position of elastic

H

Lining
Cut two
White fabric (e.g. velvet)

C

G

X

One square represents 2.5cm (1in)

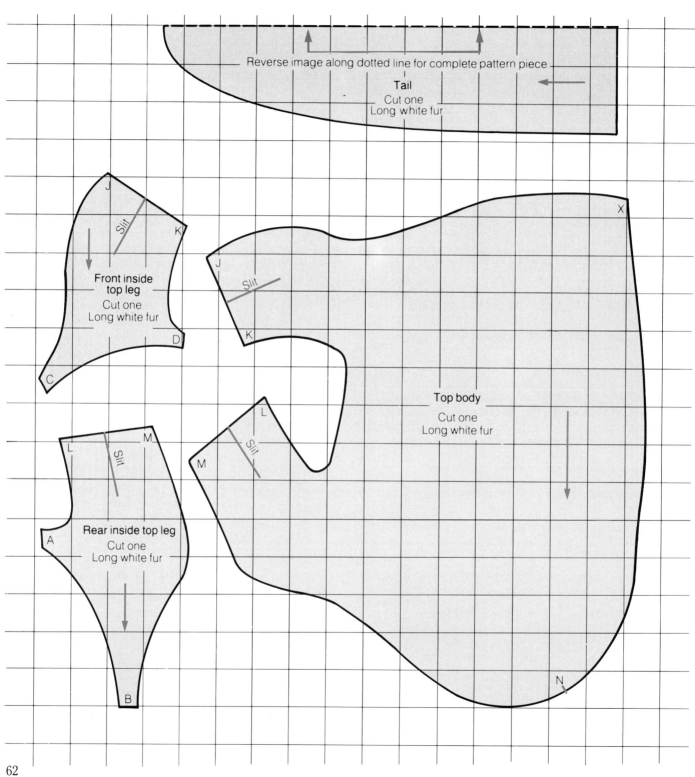

Reverse image along dotted line for complete pattern piece

Tail
Cut one
Long white fur

J

Slit

K

**Front inside
top leg**
Cut one
Long white fur

D

C

J

Slit

K

X

Top body
Cut one
Long white fur

L

M

Slit

L

Slit

M

A

Rear inside top leg
Cut one
Long white fur

B

N

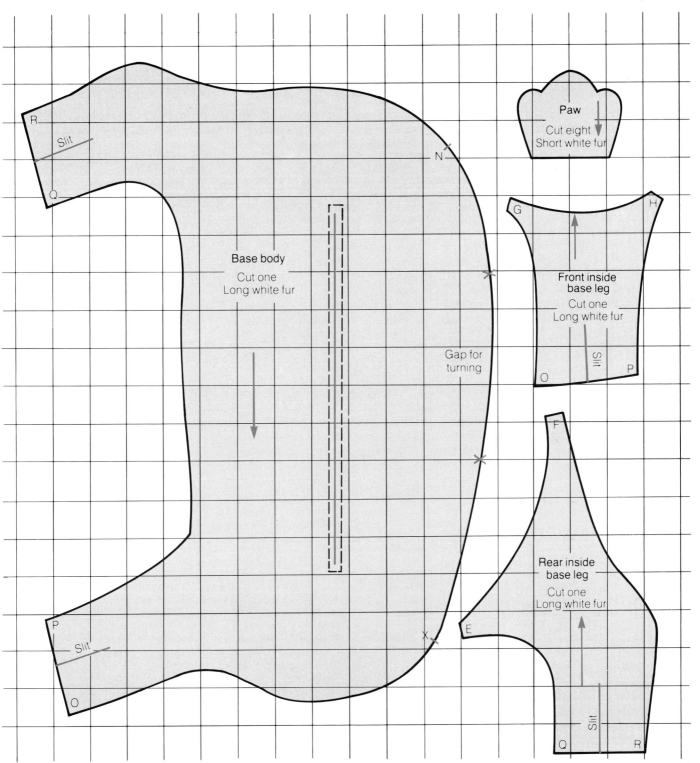

Paw
Cut eight
Short white fur

Base body
Cut one
Long white fur

Gap for
turning

Front inside
base leg
Cut one
Long white fur

Rear inside
base leg
Cut one
Long white fur

Slit

Slit

Slit

Slit

R
Q
P
O
N
G
H
O
P
F
E
X
Q
R

INDEX

KNITTING ABBREVIATIONS

K	knit	dec	decrease
P	purl	inc	increase
RS	right side	beg	beginning
WS	wrong side	rem	remaining
st	stitch	foll	following
sts	stitches	cont	continue
st st	stocking stitch	alt	alternate
	stitch	patt	pattern

ACKNOWLEDGEMENTS

Roller blind supplied by Sunway Blinds Ltd., UK.
Fimo modelling material supplied by Inscribe Ltd., UK.
White cane chair supplied by Wesley Barrell, UK.
Upholstery by David Scotcher, UK.

Special thanks also go to Madonna, Morris Minor,
Muswell (alias Spats) and Rosalinda for their
cooperation and charm during the photography.